Journey Around Cape Cod

& the Islands from A to Z

by Martha Day Zschock

COMMONWEALTH EDITIONS

Originally published 1999 in hardcover by Covered Bridge Press
ISBN 1-58066-025-8
First Commonwealth Editions hardcover 2001
ISBN 978-1-889833-28-6
First paperback edition 2008
ISBN 978-1-933212-94-4

Commonwealth Editions is the trade imprint of Memoirs Unlimited, Inc.,
266 Cabot Street, Beverly, Massachusetts 01915.
Visit us on the Web at www.commonwealtheditions.com.
Visit Martha Zschock on the Web at www.journeyaround.com.
10 9 8 7 6 5 4 3 2 1

Printed in Korea

To

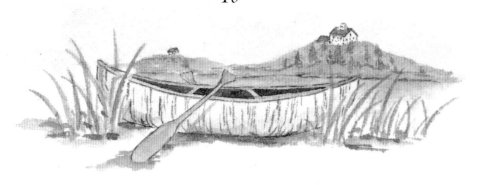

my wonderful family

and to my friends at

Hyannis East Elementary School

Greetings, my friends, and welcome to Cape Cod and the Islands!

Cape Cod—the fragile arm of land jutting eastward out into the Atlantic, together with Martha's Vineyard and Nantucket—has an interesting past and from the looks of things, an interesting future. Cape Cod has a story for everyone.

Indian legends tell us that the giant "Maushop" created these lands. History books record that the English explorer, Sir Bartholomew Gosnold, named the Cape after the huge number of fish he caught in the bay. There are stories of Native Americans living here peacefully long before any settlers arrived and, of course, the Pilgrims first landed here before moving on to Plymouth. For the adventurous, stories of pirates and sunken treasures abound. Rumors are told of "mooncussers" who lured ships to shore with lanterns and then robbed them of their bounty.

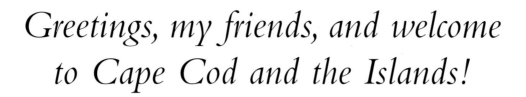

There is much to explore, so come and let's take a journey around Cape Cod.

Once Cape Cod sand gets into your shoes...

you will always return!

Ages ago, all traders arrived at Aptucxet.

Cape Cod Bay

Pilgrims from Plymouth

Old Scusset Creek

Indians from Cape Cod

Old Manomet River

Dutch from New York

Buzzard's Bay

Built by the Pilgrims in 1627, the Aptucxet Trading Post was the first trading post in this area. Furs, tools, cloth and other goods were traded. Wampum beads were used as money. Purple beads were worth twice as much as white ones.

Indians called squash, corn, and beans the "three sisters" because they took care of each other. Beans grew up the corn and squash shaded the roots.

Aptucxet Trading Post, Bourne

Boats bring barges beneath Bourne Bridge.

The great arm of the Cape was long and dangerous to sail around. The need for a canal was recognized by the Pilgrims and looked into by George Washington. In 1914, the Cape Cod Canal was completed, connecting Buzzard's Bay and Cape Cod Bay. Later it was widened, making it the world's widest sea level canal. The U.S. Army Corps of Engineers maintains the canal today.

Figure out the secret message spelled in code flags used by boaters.

Bourne Bridge, Bourne
Headquarters, Cape Cod Canal Field Office, Buzzard's Bay

Cape Codders crave cranberries to cure colds.

Cranberries grow in moist areas called bogs. In the fall, the bogs are wet or dry harvested. Long ago, sailors brought barrels of nutritious cranberries with them on their voyages to prevent them from getting a disease called scurvy. Indians made pemmican with them. It was a mixture of deer meat, cranberries and fat—this country's first energy bar!

Settlers called cranberries "crane berries" after the bird that the blossoms resembled. The Indian name was "ibimi."

Cranberry Bog, Harwich

D

affodils
dance in
downtown
displays.

According to the judges, this is a perfect daffodil.

In late April, over two million daffodils bloom in Nantucket. The garden club and residents began planting them in 1974. Every spring, there's a daffodil festival with a parade of antique cars, flower shows, window displays, and picnics.

Main Street, Nantucket

Before refrigeration, salt was needed to preserve food. A reward was offered to anyone who could invent an efficient way to make salt. Captain Sears was inspired by the competition and invented a way to evaporate water from seawater leaving the salt behind. At first called "Sear's Folly," the idea caught on and his saltworks were soon seen up and down the coast of Cape Cod.

Early settlers made salt by boiling sea water until the water evaporated and the salt remained. Many forests were cut down in the process.

Aptucxet Trading Post, Bourne

F isherfolk favor fair forecasts.

The Provider, overlooking Chatham Fish Pier, is a monument dedicated to fishermen. Everyday local fleets return to unload their catch. It's a good time for folks and sea gulls to pick up their dinner.

Blue fish, bass, flounder, haddock, tuna and (of course) cod are some of the many fish caught in Cape Cod waters. Commercial fishing is mostly done with nets.

Rock Harbor, Orleans
Fish Pier, Chatham

Gristmills grind grain.

The Stoney Brook Gristmill sits on the foundation of an earlier mill and was built using wood recycled from old saltworks. The area was once called Factory Village where everything from ice cream to overalls was produced.

Every spring, thousands of herring swim up Stoney Brook from the bay to spawn in the ponds behind the mill.

Stoney Brook Gristmill, Brewster

Hearths heated historic homes.

Half House

Three Quarter House

Full House

Some say that the Hoxie House is the oldest house on Cape Cod, but that's hard to prove. Built in the traditional saltbox style, it has two stories in front, a central chimney and a long sloping roof in the back. The original owners had thirteen children who all slept in a loft above the kitchen.

Long ago, children's toys were mostly homemade like this cornhusk doll.

Hoxie House, Sandwich

I yannough's image illustrates his importance.

The Indians living on Cape Cod were peaceful and accepted the Pilgrims who landed on their shores. Settlers, however, were often suspicious of the Indians' unfamiliar ways. They displaced many Indians and the deadly plague they brought killed many more. At the Mashpee Indian Meeting House, the Tribal Council works to preserve and celebrate their Native American heritage.

Arrowhead

Paint pot

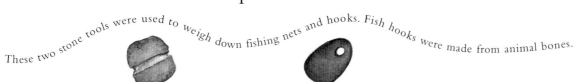
These two stone tools were used to weigh down fishing nets and hooks. Fish hooks were made from animal bones.

Main St. Village Green, Hyannis
Indian Meeting House, Mashpee

J

arves' jewel-tone glass brings joy to collectors.

The Boston and Sandwich Glass Factory was established in 1825 by Deming Jarves who believed the area's natural resources (trees and sand) to be perfect for making glass. The local sand, however, was unsuitable and another kind of sand had to be imported from elsewhere. Today, all that remains is a plaque near the boardwalk to Town Beach and the valuable works of art cherished by collectors.

Sandwich Glass Museum, Sandwich
Town Beach, Sandwich

Pairpoint glassworks in Sagamore carries on the tradition of blown glass. It's fun to watch.

Kettle ponds were created as glaciers crept northward.

Glacier

Imbedded Ice Chunk

Ice Melted to Form Kettle Ponds

Rising ground water filled kettles

Scientists have determined that kettle ponds were formed from deposits left by the glacier that once covered Cape Cod. In the case of Scargo Lake, however, Indian legends hold different theories about how *this* particular pond was formed.

There are several versions of the Indian legend about Princess Scargo. In one, she was given a pumpkin filled with fish by a suitor. To save her people after a drought, the lake was dug with clam shells and Princess Scargo poured her fish into it. In another, the suitor who could shoot an arrow across the lake would marry her.

Scargo Lake and Tower, Dennis

Lanterns lit
Lighthouses
long ago.

Lighthouses warn ships of dangers from sandbars, rocks and ledges. Lighthouses used to have keepers who were responsible for keeping the lanterns lit. Today, they are lit with electricity and their beacons can be seen 20-30 miles away. Each lighthouse has its own unique flashes, color, and sound.

Nauset Light and Highland Light (in Truro) had to be moved back because of erosion.

Many other Cape and Island lighthouses will be washed away unless they are moved.

Nauset Light, Eastham

Methodist members met in Martha's Vineyard.

Oak Bluffs began as a religious summer camp meeting ground in 1835. People began to build cottages on their camp sites and tried to "out do" their neighbors with ornate decorations. The highlight of the summer is Illumination Night when the hundreds of cottages are lit with Oriental lanterns that create a fairytale wonderland.

During the summer, religious services and weekly sing-alongs take place in the central tabernacle.

Camp Grounds, Oak Bluffs

Narratives on nature were written at Nauset.

Herring Gull

Spotted Sandpiper

Starfish

Steamer

Moonsnail

Scallop

Piping Plover

Sea Urchin

Sand Dollar

Mussel

Henry Beston spent the year of 1926 to 1927 writing about nature in his remote house, Fo'castle, on the spit of land dividing Nauset Marsh and the Atlantic Ocean. Upon his return, his fiancée, who believed strongly in his work, declared, "No book, no marriage." His famous book, *The Outermost House*, was published the following year. The house was lost to a storm in 1978.

Cape Codders make jelly out of beach plums. Settlers made candles from the waxy bayberry plant. This took a long time.

Coast Guard Beach, Eastham

Osprey's original habitat is becoming obsolete.

Ospreys look for dead trees along marshes on which to build their half-ton nests. Increased development along the coastline, however, has made good nesting sites harder to find. The phone and electric companies and nature preservation groups have joined forces to help ospreys by erecting nesting platforms made out of telephone poles and wire cable spools.

Ospreys lay between two and four speckled eggs. They hatch in five to six weeks.

Osprey Nest, Nauset Marsh, Orleans

Pilgrims persevered with prayer and patience.

Pilgrims first landed in Provincetown after their long and difficult voyage. It was here that they signed the Mayflower Compact before moving on to Plymouth. The Pilgrim Monument was built in 1910 as a tribute to the Pilgrims; it is the tallest granite structure in America.

The Pilgrims found some Indian corn stored in the sand in Truro. The area today is called "Corn Hill" and a plaque marks the spot.

Pilgrim Monument, Provincetown

CHOWDER

Quahogs are a hardy clam and will flourish under almost any condition. Every Cape Cod shellfisherperson will give you his or her version of just the right way to harvest them. They are a staple ingredient in the well-loved New England clam chowder. A clambake would be incomplete without at least a cup full.

clam rings protect quahogs from being over harvested. No clam may be taken under 2″. Clams 2-2¹/₄″ are called littlenecks, 2¹/₄″-3″ are cherrystones, 3″ and up are "chowders."

Quissett Harbor, Falmouth

Rescuers ran after wrecks.

Shifting sandbars along the Outer Cape (nicknamed "Graveyard of Ships") presented a great danger to sailors. By 1880, shipwrecks averaged one every two weeks. Patrols were established to watch for ships in danger. The motto of the brave rescuers was, "You have to go out, but you don't have to come back."

Today lifeguards watch for swimmers in trouble during the summer.

Highland Light, Truro

Whaling voyages were dangerous and lasted many years. When a whale was spotted, small harpooning boats were sent after it. Once speared, the whale led the men on a "Nantucket sleigh ride" that lasted until the whale became tired out. The blubber from the whales was melted into valuable oil used in lamps.

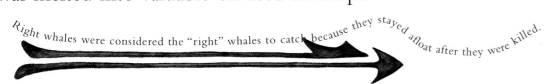

Right whales were considered the "right" whales to catch because they stayed afloat after they were killed.

Whaling Museum, Nantucket

Trains took tourists to the tip.

"TOURISTS"
by
CHAIM GROSS

1887 CHATHA

Trains advanced industry and tourism on Cape Cod during the 1800's. When the canal was built, a railroad bridge was constructed that could be lowered to allow trains to cross, and raised to let boats pass underneath.

← Dennis

Many of the old railroad beds are now part of the "rail trail" enjoyed by bikers.

Railroad Museum, Chatham
Commercial Street, Provincetown

Wellfleet →

Under Uncle Tim's Bridge live unspoiled marshes.

Marshes serve as nursery schools for sea life. Many varieties of clams, crabs, and fish make their homes in these safe, protected areas away from the harsh ocean waves. When marshland is filled and developed, these creatures have no place to go.

When a hermit crab outgrows its shell, it has to look for a new one. It cannot grow its own.

Uncle Tim's Bridge, Wellfleet

Visitor Centers offer vast views.

CAPE COD NATIONAL SEASHORE
UNITED STATES DEPARTMENT OF THE INTERIOR
NATIONAL PARK SERVICE

NATIONAL PARK SERVICE

DEPARTMENT OF THE INTERIOR

President Kennedy signed a bill that established the Cape Cod National Seashore Park in 1961. The park covers 27,000 acres of land from Chatham to Provincetown. This land is protected from development and is preserved for all to enjoy in years to come.

The Buttonbush Trail in Eastham has signs written in Braille and has markers that help people who can't see.

Salt Pond Visitor Center, Eastham

When winds whirl, wind-mills work.

The Eastham Windmill is the oldest windmill on Cape Cod. It was floated across the bay from Plymouth in 1793. The roofs of many windmills could turn. Horses or oxen pulled a wheel and pole attached to the roof in order to adjust the sails that powered the mill.

Settlers loved honey on their cornbread which was made with corn ground in the mill.

Route 6, Eastham

EXcitement at X-mas strolls.

Festive Christmas Strolls were dreamed up by Cape Cod and Island towns to encourage people to visit in the winter time. Burning a bayberry candle to the socket on New Year's Eve is said to bring "health to the home and wealth to the pocket."

It takes about 12-15 pounds of bayberries to make 1 pound of wax—this was a time consuming process.

Main Street, Nantucket

Y armouth pump yields water year-round.

Village pumps were important in early Cape Cod times when people had no running water in their houses. In 1928 Mrs. Simpkins donated the beautiful wrought iron arc over the Yarmouth Pump to the town in memory of her husband who loved animals.

Sea Lavender
(Beach Heather)

Endangered means almost extinct. Threatened means almost endangered. Thanks to the efforts of conservationist groups, many plants and animals are making a comeback.

Lady
Slipper

Route 6A, Yarmouth

Zooplankton is zapped up by whales.

Today Cape Codders have turned their efforts to saving whales, an animal group they once helped to deplete. Scientists study the migration of whales using the markings on their flukes. Whale watches are a favorite activity for many Cape Cod vacationers.

Seals and dolphins can also be seen swimming in Cape Cod waters. Dolphins sometimes like to surf in the waves made by whale watching boats.

Whale Watch, Provincetown